Mother's Cook Book

Traditional European Desserts

By

Rea-Silvia Steliana Costin, P.E.

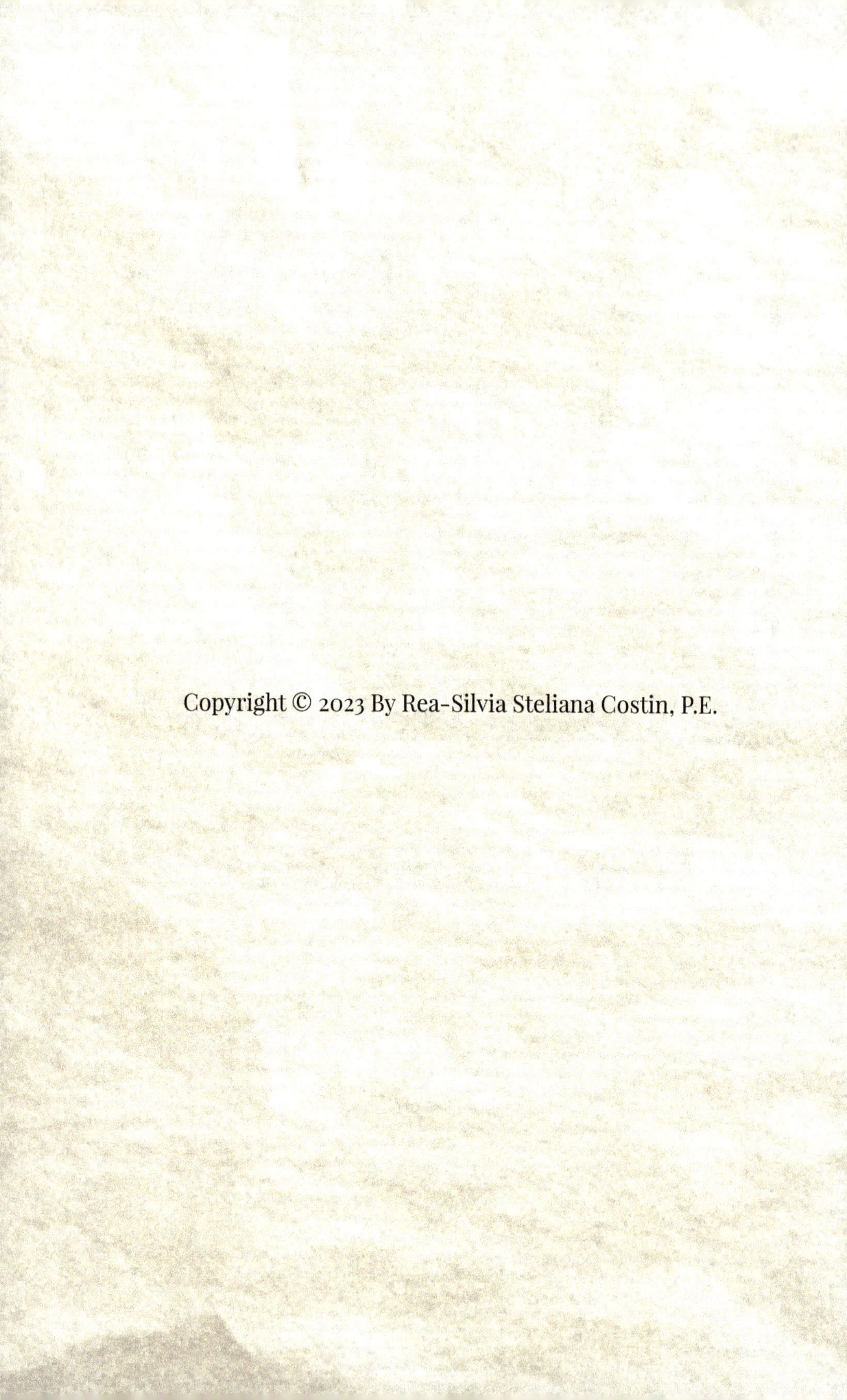

This book is dedicated to the memory of my mother, Steliana Costin, who was a teacher of the culinary art.

As, a child, I always thought of my mother as belonging to us, the family, entirely. Could not imagine that she had a separate life as a teacher, and loved and formed young people to become fruitful citizens of society. I was only seeing one side of mother's persona.

The first glimpse of who my mother was happened when we were in vacation hiking throughout a small village in the Carpathian Mountains and logging with a peasant family.

My mother talked to the young girl, dreaming of the word to open in front of her eyes, and could not find a way out of the village life. My mother told the young girl how to apply to the school she was teaching to, in Bucharest, how she can better herself, and live her dreams.

That's what teachers do, open doors, make dreams come true!

Note: *This is a very comprehensive cook book, concise, and precise, and the recipes arranged in a logical manner, by the methodology of preparation the dough.*

This book is written in metric units (the European system), but the units can be easily converted in English units with the help of a unit convertor.

Also the quantities might seem rather on an industrial scale; again, it can be reduced by dividing the quantities for as many, or as little, portions you need, and here the decimal system is a big help!

Table of Contents

Chapter VI: Pie dough 98

Chapter VII: Greek filo 104

Chapter 1: Kitchen's Deserts

Those are simple, nutritious, deserts made with whatever you already have in your pantry and your fridge.

GRITS WITH MILK

10 portions of 150 grams

Milk... 1.250 l
Grits... 250 grams
Sugar.. 150 grams
salt... 10 g
vanilla extract... 1/8 g
fruit syrup.. 250 g

Preparation: *Bring the milk to a boil, add the grits, a little bit at a time, while whisking continuously for a homogenous result, without lumps. Add the salt, the sugar and the vanilla extract while cooking at a reduced heat.*

After the grits are done, pour it in the serving plates and add the fruit syrup when cold.

GRITS WITH WHIPPED CREAM AND CANDIED FRUITS

Milk	1.5 l
Grits	200 g
Sugar	150g
Vanilla extract	1/8 g
Candied fruits	100g

for decoration

whipped cream	250g
vanilla extract	1/8g
sugar	50g

Preparation: *Boil the grits the same as the grits with syrup (above). When out of the fire add the candied fruits chopped in small cubs, and then set it up for service in plates. Let the grits cool off, then whip the cream with sugar and vanilla extract and ornate the plates.*

RICE WITH MILK

Milk	1.5l
Rice	375g
Sugar	200g
salt	10g
vanilla extract	1/8g
cinnamon	10g

Preparation: *In a saucepan boil the water, then add the rice and cook it, then add the salt and the milk and continue cooking at reduced heat until the rice is completely cooked and tender. Add the sugar and the vanilla extract and continue cooking for about 10 more minutes at reduced heat. Place it in the serving plates. When almost cooled, add the cinnamon on top.*

RICE A LA RUSE

Milk	1.5l
Rice	350g
Sugar	200g
Vanillas extract	1/8g
Salt	10g

for decorum

wiped cream	250g
sugar	50g
candied fruits	100g
vanilla extract	1/8g
fruit syrup	150g

Prepare the rice in the same manner as the rice with milk above. After it has cooled off add the fruit syrup. Decorate the serving plates with whipped cream and candied fruits cut in small cubes.

RICE WITH ORANGES

Milk	1.5l
Rice	300g
Sugar	300g
vanilla extract	1/8g
oranges	750g
whipped cream	300g

Preparation: *In a Dutch pan boil the milk, the rice, with half the quantity of the sugar and the vanilla extract.*

Let it cool, then mixed it with 1/3 of the whipping cream. Set it in a round serving plate, in form of a mount.

½ of the orange peel (without the white part), wash it first in scalded water to eliminate the bitterness, then boil it with the syrup made with the other half of the sugar quantity.

Slice the peeled oranges in thin slices (Julien) and arrange them around the rice, then add the Julien cut orange peels and the syrup around the edges. Add the remaining whipped cream in the middle of the rice mount.

RICE WITH CHARLOTTE

Milk.. 1.5l
Rice 250g
Vanillas extract 1/8g
Sugar... 100g
Raisins.. 50g
Candied fruits.................................... 100g

for charlotte

eggs.. 2each
sugar 150g
milk.. 150ml
gelatin.. 6 sheets
whipped cream 300g

Preparation: *Boil the rice as in the rice with milk recipe (above). Let it cool off and mix it with the raisins and the candied fruits cut in small cubes.*

Prepare the charlotte as follow:

In a bowl, beat the eggs and the sugar, and then add the milk. Pour the mixture in a pan and on the stove while continuously whisking until boils. Take it out of the stove and add the gelatin that was previously dissolved in cold water. After cooling add the whipped cream.

Mix the charlotte with the cooled rice and set it in a form. After the composition is set in the form turn the form upside down into a plateau.

COTTAGE CHEESE BALLS

Cottage cheese.. 1kg
Grits 100g
Flour 150g
Eggs .... 3 each
butter 250g
sour cream... 500g
sugar 200g
salt.. 50g

Preparation: *In a large bowl mix the cottage cheese with the yolks, the grits that were boiled and cooled, the salt, the flour and the eggs whites that were whipped in soft picks. Form in round balls or by using a spoon and boil them in salted boiled water, at medium heat, for about 10 minutes until they rise to the surface. Spoon them out of the water and place them on a plateau. Sprinkle the sugar in top of them and 1/3 of the butter and put them in the oven for 5 minutes. Serve them with sour cream and the remaining melted butter.*

FRIED COTTAGE CHEESE PATTIES WITH SOUR CREAM (PAPANASI)

Cottage cheese...1kg
Flour 500g
Eggs ....4 each
Sugar...150g
Salt...10g
lemon zest..10g
baking powder 1g
sour cream...500g
oil..150g

Preparation: *Mix the cottage cheese with the salt, eggs yolks, flour, and lemon zest, ¼ of sugar quantity, the eggs whites beaten to soft peaks, and the baking powder. Portion, and form it in balls (2 balls per one serving portion). Roll the balls in flour and then pat them in patties. Then fry the patties in hot oil in the frying pan. Serve them hot, with powder sugar and sour cream.*

POTATOES BALLS WITH PRUNES

10 serving portions of 250g each

Potatoes	2kg
Flour	500g
Eggs	3 each
Salt	50g
Prunes	1kg
lard	250g
bread crumbs	250g
sugar	250g
sugar	250g
cinnamon	1/4g

Preparation: *wash the potatoes, and boil them whole. Then peel them and let them cool. Purée the potatoes and mix it with the eggs, salt and flour, then knead the dough. Spread the dough in 1 to 1 ½ cm thickness and cut it in squares, counting 5 to 6 per serving portion.*

Prepare the prunes by washing them and coring them, and by placing a bit of sugar inside.

Place a prune in the middle of the potatoes square dough and close it by making it a ball. Place them on side until all quantity is ready, and then boil them in salted boiling water for about 10 minutes or until the potato balls rise to the surface.

Prepare the bread crumbs by roasting them in a pan with the hot lard.

Get the potatoes rolls out of the boiling water, dry them, and roll them in the roasted crumbs. Then arrange them on a tray, sprinkle them with powdered sugar and cinnamon and place them in the oven for an additional 5 minutes.

POTATOES BATONS

10 serving portions of 300g each

Potatoes	3kg
Flour	700g
Eggs	5 each
Salt	5g
lard	250g
bread crumbs	250g
sugar	250g

Preparation: *prepare the potatoes dough the same as for the potatoes balls (see above). Form it in form of batons. Boil them the same way as for the potatoes balls (see above), until they rise to the boiling water surface, drain them and roll them in the roasted bread crumbs. Add the sugar before serving.*

BEIGNETS (MICSUNELE)

Flour 750g
Eggs .... 4 each
Rom 25ml
Sour cream 250g
salt 5g
vanilla sugar 150g
vanilla extract 1/8g
oil 200ml

Preparation: *in a bowl mix the flour (sieved), eggs, ¼ sugar, sour cream and salt. Knead the dough well, and then let it rest for 10 minutes. Using a rolling pin spared the dough in a thin layer on the working surface. Cut it in slices with the cutting roll in form of a rhomb. Then cut the rhomb in the middle and tread one corner through the hole. Fry them in hot oil, and serve them with powdered sugar and vanilla sugar.*

FLAN (CARAMEL SUGAR CREAM)

Eggs	8each
Sugar	500g
Milk	1l
vanilla baton	1/8g
rom	50ml

Preparation: *In a Dutch oven pan burn 1/3 of the sugar quantity and coat evenly the bottom and sides of the pan by swirling the caramel sugar around.*

On a bowl whisk the eggs, sugar and vanilla until homogenous, then add the milk, a bit at a time, whisking continuously until the sugar is completely dissolved.

Pour the composition in the Dutch oven pan already prepared, and bake it in a Bain marine in the oven for 45 minutes.

When completely cooled, turn the flan over on the serving plate. Slice it, and serve it with the sauce from the caramel sugar and rom.

BIRD'S MILK

10 portions of 200g each

```
Eggs ............................................................ 7 each
Sugar........................................................... 300g
milk............................................................. 2l
vanilla ......................................................... 1/8g
```

Preparation: *Boil the milk with 1/3 of the sugar quantity and vanilla. Separate the yolks from the eggs whites. Beat the eggs whites with 1/3 of the sugar quantity to hard picks. Take spoonful sizes of the beaten eggs whites and place them in the boiling milk and boil them for 3 minutes at reduce heat (turn them around at half time). Spoon the balls on a plate.*

In a separate bowl whisk the eggs yolks with the remaining sugar and vanilla. Thin the mixture with the cooled milk, and then put the mixture again on the stove and boil it for 5 minutes while continuously whisking Let it cool and serve it with the white eggs balls on top of the sauce.

APPLE SOUFFLÉ

Flour	*250g*
Eggs	*3 each*
Sugar	*75g*
Milk	*100ml*
Apples	*1kgrasberry*
cinnamon	*7g*
oil	*200ml*
raspberry syrup	*150g*
salt	*5g*

Preparation: *In a bowl, sieve the flour and mix it with the eggs yolks, salt, and milk. Separately beat the eggs whites with ½ of the sugar quantity and fold it gently within the composition.*

Peel the apples, core, and slice them. Powder the apple slices with cinnamon powder, dredge them through the composition, and then fry them in hot oil.

Serve the apple slices hot, with raspberry syrup and sugar.

COTTAGE CHEESE STRUDEL

Flour *350g*
Salt.. *15g*
Butter.. *125g*
Oil.. *25ml*

filling

cottage cheese.. *600g*
sugar *150g*
vanillin.. *1/8g*
lemon zest.. *25g*
Eggs .... *3 each*
Flour *75g*
Powder sugar *75g*

Preparation: *Sieve the flour on the working surface; add the salt the butter and water as necessary to form dough. Let it rest for 20 to 30 minutes. Add some flour to the working surface and spread the dough in a thin layer using a rolling pin, or your hands. Sprinkle oil in top of it.*

Filling: *In a bowl mix the cottage cheese, eggs, flour, sugar, lemon zest and vanillin.*

Cut the dough in pieces the length of the baking tray. Set the filling on each dough strip and roll it making sure you tack in the ends as you roll. Place the rolls on the tray, and brush them with melted butter. Bake them at moderate heat.

Serve it sprinkled with powder sugar.

APPLE STRUDEL

Flow 350g
Butter 125g
Oil 25ml
Salt 10g

filling

apples 1,250kg
sugar 150g
bread crumbs 100g
vanillin 1/8g
Cinnamon 2g
Powder sugar 75g

Preparation: *the preparation is the same as for the cottage cheese strudel.*

For the filling: *peel and core the apples, shred them, and mix it with the bread crumbs, cinnamon and vanillin. Add the sugar at the end.*

Everything else is the same as for the cottage cheese strudel.

CREPES WITH COTTAGE CHEESE AND SOUR CREAM

10 portions of 250g each

Flour	500g
Eggs	4 each
Milk	500ml
Sugar	100g
Vanillin	1/8g
salt	10g
oil	200ml
cottage cheese	500g
sour cream	500g

Preparation: *in a bowl, sieve the flour and mix it with the eggs, salt, 1/3 of the sugar quantity, ½ of vanillin, and some milk. Mix the composition well until homogenous. Thin the composition with milk.*

In a nonstick frying pan, heat the oil (one teaspoon for each crepe), pour one small laden of the composition into the pan, and swirl it around until the composition covers the entire pan's bottom, Fry the crepe on one side then turn it around, either by flipping the pan, or using a spatula.

Place the crepes on a plate until all are done

For the filling, mix the cottage cheese with the remaining sugar and vanillin, fill each crepe an roll it making sure you tack the edges inside as you roll, then place the rolls on a yean vase.

Add the sour cream on top and put it in the oven for 15 to 20 minutes.

CREPES WITH JAM

10 portions of 120g each

Flour 500g
Eggs .... 4 each
Milk 500ml
Salt 10g
Powder sugar 100g
sugar 250g
jam 250g
vanillin 1/8g
lard 150g

Preparation: Prepare the crepes the same as for the crepes with cottage cheese (see above), then fill them, while hot, with jam an close them in form of a square envelope. Serve them with powder sugar.

CREPES PUDDING WITH COTTAGE CHEESE AND VANILLA SAUCE

For the crepes

Flour	200g
Eggs	2 each
Milk	400ml
Sugar	25g
Salt	10g
Oil	50ml

For the filling

Cottage cheese	300g
Vanillin	1/8g
Sugar	50g
For the tray Butter	25g
Sugar	50g

for the composition

milk	600ml
corn starch	50g
eggs	2 each
vanillin	1/8g
sugar	150g

for the sauce

milk	250ml
sugar	50g
corn starch	10g
vanillin	1/8g

Preparation: *Prepare the crepes and the filling the same as for the crepes with cottage cheese (see above), roll the crepes making sure you tack in the ends as you roll, and set them in a tray coated with butter and sugar.*

Pour on top of the crepes the composition prepared as such: boil the milk; add the sugar, the vanillin, and the corn starch that was previously dissolved in a bit of cold milk.

Let it thicken while continuously whisking. Let it cool and mix it with the beaten eggs.

Pour the composition on top of the crepes and set the tray in the oven. Bake it for 20 minutes at medium heat.

Let it cool and cut it in portions.

Serve it with the vanilla sauce that was prepared form the sugar, vanillin and corn starch boiled in milk for 10 minutes.

BREAD PUDDING WITH VINE SAUCE

10 portions of 200g each

French bread	*550g*
Milk	*750ml*
Sugar	*250g*
Butter	*100g*
raisins	*50g*
candied fruits	*150g*
eggs	*6 each*
vanillin	*1/8g*

For souse

Eggs	*3 each*
Sugar	*125g*
vine	*300ml*
vanillin	*1/8 gr*

Preparation: *Cut the crust out of the French bread, and cut it in small cubs. Place them in a large bowl. Boil the milk with the ½ of the sugar quantity and vanillin. Pour the hot milk over the bread cubs and let it soak. When cooled, mix it with the eggs yolks, vanillin, raisins, the candied fruits (Cut in small pieces), the rest of the sugar and the beaten eggs whites.*

Pour the composition in a tray that was smeared with butter, and bake it for 30 to 40 minutes at moderate heat. When ready, cut it in square pieces and serve it with vine sauce (shadou).

For the vine sauce (shadou): mix the eggs yolks with the sugar and vanillin, and thin it with the vine. Boil it until thickens, making sure you whisk continuous.

GRITS PUDDING WITH VINE SAUCE

10 portions of 200 g each

Grits	300g
Milk	1,350l
Sugar	200g
Vanillin	1/8g
Eggs	3 each
Salt	10g
butter	50g
crumbs	50g

for the vine sauce

eggs	2 each
sugar	100g
white vine	250ml

Preparation: *boil the grits with the milk and ½ of the sugar quantity and salt (Same as in Grits with milk–see above). Let it cool then mix it with the rest of the sugar quantity, vanillin, yolks, and the beaten eggs whites. Pour the composition into a yen form that was coated with butter and bread crumbs. Bake it at medium heat for 40 minutes.*

Serve it with vine sauce that is prepared the same as in the bread pudding recipe (see above).

RICE PUDDING WITH APPLES

10 portions of 250g each

Milk 1l
Rice 750g
Sugar 350g
Eggs .... 5 each
Apples 1kg
butter 50g
crumbs 50g
vanillin 1/8g
salt 20g
fruits syrup 250g

Preparation: boil the rice in some water until opens, then add the milk and boil at reduced heat. Let it cool. In a bowl mix the yolks with ½ of the sugar quantity, salt and vanilla, then mix it with the rice, and the eggs whites beaten to soft picks and the remaining sugar.

Place the composition on a tray (coated with butter and bread crumbs) in layers, 3 layers of rice and 2 layers of apples (that were peeled, cored, and cut in thin slices). Bake at medium heat for 30 minutes. Let it cool, cut it in pieces, and serve with the fruit syrup, or vine sauce.

NOODLES PUDDING WITH VANILLA SAUCE

For the noodles

Flour	200g
Eggs	2 each
Salt	20g

Composition

Eggs	2 each
Sugar	200g
Vanillin	1/8g
Milk	1l

for the form

butter	25g
crumbs	50g

sauce

eggs	2 each
sugar	50g
corn starch	10g
milk	250ml
Vanillin	1/8g

Preparation: *Prepare the filo for the noodles mixing flour (sieved), salt, eggs and water. Work the dough good and then let it rest for 15 minutes. Spread the dough in a thin layer and let it rest.*

Roll it and cut it in thin strips. Boil the milk with the vanillin and 2/3 of the sugar quantity and add the noodles (make sure you shake the excess flour). Let it cool. Mix it with the yolks, the rest of the sugar, and the beaten eggs whites. Pour the composition on a tray coated with butter and crumbs.

Bake it at medium heat for 30 minutes.

Serve it with vanilla syrup prepared from milk, sugar, corn starch, vanillin and eggs that you boil until thickens and cool.

VANILLA SHUFFLE

Milk.. 1l
Sugar... 500g
Butter.. 150g
Powder sugar 150g
flour 300g
eggs.. 15 each
vanillin... 1/8g

Preparation: *Boil the milk with 2/3 of the sugar quantity, vanillin, and 2/3 of the butter.*

In a bowl, mix the flour and the yolks and pour over the boiled milk, while continuous whisking for a homogeny composition, without lumps. Let it cool off.

Fold in the eggs whites that were beaten with the rest of the sugar.

Pour the composition into forms (gratin) coated with butter. Bake them at medium heat for 20 minutes.

Serve the shuffle in the forms that you baked them in, immediately after you took them out of the Oven, and powder them with powder sugar.

Chapter II: Semi-fabricates

Semi-fabricates are produces that are used in finalizing other products. Sometimes they are used as final product.

BAROT OF GRILLED ALMONDS

    Almonds 450g
    sugar 650g

Preparation: *place the almonds on a tray and grill them in the Owen.*

On a pan melt /burn the sugar. Pour the burned sugar over the baked almonds and place it on a marble surface that was coated with butter. Let it cool and cut it in small pieces.

The almonds can be substitute with peanuts (make sure you clean off all membranes')

BAROT OF FISTIC

    Almonds 3kg
    color 2g

Put the almonds on a tray and bake them until you can peel off the membranes. Then cut them in small pieces. Them place the crumbs in a vase and add the green color. Mix it well until the color is uniform.

Spread the composition on a tray in even thickness and let it dry in a warm and dry place. Use it for decorations or as a barot.

BAROT WITH GRILLED PECANS

Pecans shelled 450g
sugar 650g

Preparation: *in a try grill the pecans in the Owen until membranes are loosened. Burn the sugar in a pan and then pour it over the grilles pecans, preferable on a marble surface coated with butter.*

Cut it in pieces.

All barots are kept in glass containers, hermetic closed at temperature between 15 and 20 degrees Celsius.

CHOCOLATE BAROT

White fondant.. 800g
Powder sugar 300g
Flour 25g
cacao 50g
caramel sugar 10g

Preparation: *Sprinkle the flour on the working surface, and knead the white fondant with the cacao, powder sugar and caramel sugar until hardens. Shred it, and then spread it on a thin layer on parchment paper until dries off.*

WHITE BLAT

Eggs .... 36 each
Flour .... 1.3 kg
sugar 950
oil.. 50g

Preparation: *Separate the yolks from the eggs whites and place them in two separate bowls. Beat the yolks with ¾ of the sugar quantity until all the sugar crystals are dissolved, and yolks change color and increase in volume. In the yolks mixture add, a little at a time, 200ml water, while beaten.*

In a separate bowl, beat the eggs whites, add the remaining sugar toward the end and continue beating to hard picks.

Fold in the eggs whites with the yolks and add the flour (sieved). Fold in gently until the composition is uniform (without any lumps). At the end add the oil.

Coat the bottom of the metal forms with parchment paper that was coated with butter on both sides. Bake it, first at reduce heat, then at medium heat.

Taste it for readiness with a tooth pick (it should be clean when ready).

BLAT FOR THE TORTE

Result 10 tortes of 270g each

Eggs	36 each
Flour	1.3kg
sugar	950g
oil	50ml

Preparation: *is the same as for white blat (see above). The Composition is poured in spring metallic forms with the bottoms covered in parchment paper and put on trays to bake in Owen.*

CACAO BLAT

Eggs	36 each
Flour	1.250kg
Sugar for caramel	100g
sugar	850g
cacao	50g
oil	50g

Preparation: *is the same as for the white blat (see above) with the difference that the yolks are colored by adding the caramel sugar, and the flour is mixed with the cacao before adding it to the composition.*

COCOA BLAT WITH ALMONDS

Eggs .... 36 each
Flour 1.2kg
Cacao 50g
Oil.. 50g
sugar 850g
almonds 250g
caramel sugar 100g

Preparation: *is the same as for the cacao blat (see above) with the difference that the flour is mixed with the grounded almonds.*

CHOCOLATE BLAT

Eggs .... 36 each
Flour 1.3kg
Oil.. 50ml
sugar .... 900 g
caramel sugar 100g

Preparation: *it is the same as for the cacao blat (see above) with the difference that the composition is colored with the caramel sugar.*

BLAT WITH PECANS

Result 3.3 kg

Eggs .... 36 each
Flour 1.20kg
Oil.. 50g
sugar 900g
pecans 250g

Preparation: *It is the same as for the white blat with the difference the flour is mixed with ground pecans.*

KATAIFI FILLOS

Result 4 kg

Kataifi damp.. 2.5kg
Glucose 500g
sugar for the syrup... 2kg
aroma fistic 5g

Preparation: *Unravel the kataifi shreds (dough) and set it uniformly on a tray, about 3 cm thick. Sprinkle them with water and put them in the oven until golden brown.*

Then add the syrup that was prepared as such: boil the sugar with water and the glucose until it is of a syrup consistency.

Add the hot syrup over the baked Kataifi.

KRANTZ BLAT

Result 1.5 kg

Eggs	24
Butter	350g
Lemon zest	25g
sugar	450g
flour	500g

Preparation: *Separate the yoks for the eggs whites. In a bowl beat the yolks with ¾ of the sugar quantity, until it increases its volume and changes color. Add the melted butter and lemon zest, and stir with a spatula.*

In a separate bowl, beat the eggs whites in soft peaks and add the remaining sugar toward the end. Fold the beaten egg whites with the yolks mixture and add the flour (sieved).

Bake it in forms that were coated with parchment paper on the bottom, first at a reduce heat, and then at medium heat.

Use it for Krantz.

DOBOS FILLOS

Eggs 340each
Flour 3800g
Flour for the tray.. 3200g
sugar 3800g
butter for coating the trays 3150g

Preparation: *separate the yolks from the eggs whites.*

Beat the yolks with ¾ of the sugar quantity, until it increases its volume, and all sugar crystals are dissolved.

In a separate bowl, beat the eggs whites until form hard peaks. Add the remaining sugar toward the end of the process.

Fold the beaten eggs whites into the yolks mixture and add the sieved flour. Fold gently with a spatula. Set the composition in trays coated with butter and flour on all sides, uniformly in a 2 to 3 cm thickness layer. Bake them in the oven at a good heat. When ready remove them for the trays and powder them with flour. Keep them in a dry and warm place.

Use it for Dobos.

ÉCLAIR SHELLS

Result 2 kg for 100 pieces

Oil..450ml
Flour 900g
Salt..5g
eggs...36 each
water 900ml

Preparation: *In a big pot, bring the water, oil, and salt to a boil. Add the flour, and mix with a wooded spatula until homogenous, for about 5 minutes. Take it out of the heat and let it cool for a while. Add the eggs, one at the time, while continuously whisking. Put the composition in a posh with a dui and form 6 to 8 cm long éclair shells, in a tray. Bake them at a good heat in the beginning, and then reduce the heat to medium, until well baked. Keep them in a dry place covered with a damp tower until using.*

They are used for eclairs.

PROFITEROLE SHELLS

Result 800g for 20 portions

Butter...100g
Oil..100ml
Water 400ml
flour 400g
eggs...15 each
salt...5g

Preparation: *it is the same as for the éclair, with the difference that is formed in round form with the diameter of 3 cm.*

SAINT HONOREE SHELLS

Oil..65ml
Butter...65g
Eggs ....8 each
flour 240g
water 250ml

Preparation: *It is the same as for the éclair shells, with the difference that the composition is poured onto two round forms and 20 small balls.*

MERENGUE SHELLS

Eggs (20eggs whites)........................10each
Vanillin...1/8g
sugar 1kg
powder sugar 100g

Preparation: *Prepare a tray by coating it with parchment paper. First, set the sugar on the tray and warm it in the oven. In a bowl, or mixer, beat up the eggs whites and add the warm sugar, a little bit at a time, until it forms hard peaks. Pout the composition in a posh with a dui and form the merengue shells on the tray coated with parchment paper, in an elongated form with 3 curls. Finish the shells by sprinkling powder sugar on them. Set the try in a warm oven until the merengue shells dried off without changing the color.*

SAVARINS

Result 100 pieces

Flour 2.6kg
Milk.. 1.5l
Sugar.. 200g
Oil for the forms 150g
Salt... 50g
leaven 200g
eggs.. 20 each
butter... 200g
lemon zest.. 50g

Preparation: *dissolve the leaven in a little warm milk; add the salt, sugar, lemon zest, and eggs. Whisk it together, then add the flour, a little at a time while whisking until it forms air balls and then add the melted butter and knead the dough until all the butter is incorporated and the dough cleans off hands. Let it rise in a warm place. Put it in savarin forms and bake them at reduced heat first, then at a good heat. When baked, remove them out of the forms immediately.*

COFFEE SYRUP

Result 2l

Sugar.. 1.1kg
Rom.. 60ml
Vanillin.. 1/8g
chicory 200ml
water 900ml

Preparation: *boil the sugar with water until starts making big bubbles, set it aside, and add the chicory. After it cools off add the rom and the vanillin.*

FISTIC SYRUP

Sugar...1.1kg
Rom...25g
Vanillin...10g
flower water 15g
green color...2g
water 900ml

Preparation: *it is the same as for the coffee syrup only that you mix it with the flowers water and vegetables color- green.*

ORANGE'S SYRUP

Sugar..1.1 kg
Orange color 2g
Alcohol 90 degrees....................................50ml
orange zest 20g
lemon juice..2 lemons
water 900ml

Preparation: *it is the same as for the coffee syrup with the difference that you add the orange zest, orange color and the alcohol after it is cooled off.*

ROM SYRUP

Sugar...1.1kg
Lemon zest 20g
Water 900ml
rom..125ml
vanillin...10g

Preparation: *it is the same as for the other syrups only that the aroma is rom and lemon Zest.*

MOCHA CREAM WITH FONDANT

Fondant white..900g
Svartz 100ml
Ground coffee..25g
butter 1kg
vanillin...1/4g

Preparation: *whisk the butter with the fondant until creamy. Add the svartz, the ground coffee and vanillin for aroma.*

CHOCOLATE CREAM WITH FONDANT

Result 2 kg

Fondant 900g
Cacao 150g
Rom essence 2g
butter 1kg
vanillin 1/4g
alcohol 90 degrees 50ml

Preparation: *whisk the butter, add the fondant, a little at a time, while whisking. Add the cacao, vanillin, rom essence, and alcohol and continue whisking until creamy.*

CHOCOLATE CREAM WITH PRALINE

Result 2 kg

Fondant white 700g
Praline 300g
Vanillin 1/4g
Alcohol 90 degrees 50ml
butter 1kg
cacao 100g
rom essence 2ml

Preparation: *whisk the butter, add the fondant, a little at a time, until the composition is creamy, and add the cacao, vanillin, rom essence, and the alcohol. When served add the praline.*

CRÈME APPAREL CHOCOLATE

Sugar... 750g
Eggs .... 3 each
Vanillin... 1/4g
Alcohol 90degrees 50ml
milk... 250ml
cacao 20g
rom essence .... 2 ml
butter 1kg

Preparation: *Mix the eggs with the sugar, add the milk and boil it (until it glues between fingers) while whisking it continuously. Take it out of the heat; add the cacao and few cubs of butter to stop the crystallization process. After the composition cools off, add the butter and whisk the composition until it foams. Add the rom essence, alcohol and vanillin.*

CRÈME WITH CANDIED FRUITS

White fondant.. 850g
Candied fruits.. 300g
Liquid color... 1ml
butter 950g
orange essence 2g

Preparation: *whisk the butter, add the fondant a little at a time, while whisking until it creams. Add the orange color, orange essence, and the candied fruits cut in small cubes.*

CRÈME APPAREL CHOCOLATE WITH PRALINE

Sugar...400g
Milk...250ml
Praline...400g
Rom...100ml
butter..950g
eggs..4 each
cacao..40g

Preparation: *the same as for the crème apparel chocolate (see above) with the difference that it's added praline when used.*

ALMONDS CRÈME

Sugar..750g
Butter...1kg
Alcohol 90 degrees......................................50ml
Eggs...4 each
Milk..150ml
Almonds..250g

Preparation: *the preparation is the same as for the crème apparel chocolate with the difference that it is not colored and the composition is mixed with the almonds that were grilled and grounded.*

CRÈME APPAREL MOCHA

Sugar	800g
Svartz	250ml
Vanillin	1/4g
eggs	4 each
butter	1.1kg

Preparation: *Mix the eggs with the sugar and the svartz. Set it on the stove and whisk it continuously. Let it cool off and add the butter. Whisk it until foams. Add the vanillin aroma.*

FRUITS CRÈME APPAREL

Sugar	750g
Milk	250ml
Candied fruits	300g
Vanillin	1/4g
eggs	3 each
butter	850g
orange essence	1ml
liquid colors	1ml

Preparation: *it is the same as for the crème apparel chocolate with the difference that you add the candied fruits cut in small cubs.*

BOILED VANILLA CRÈME

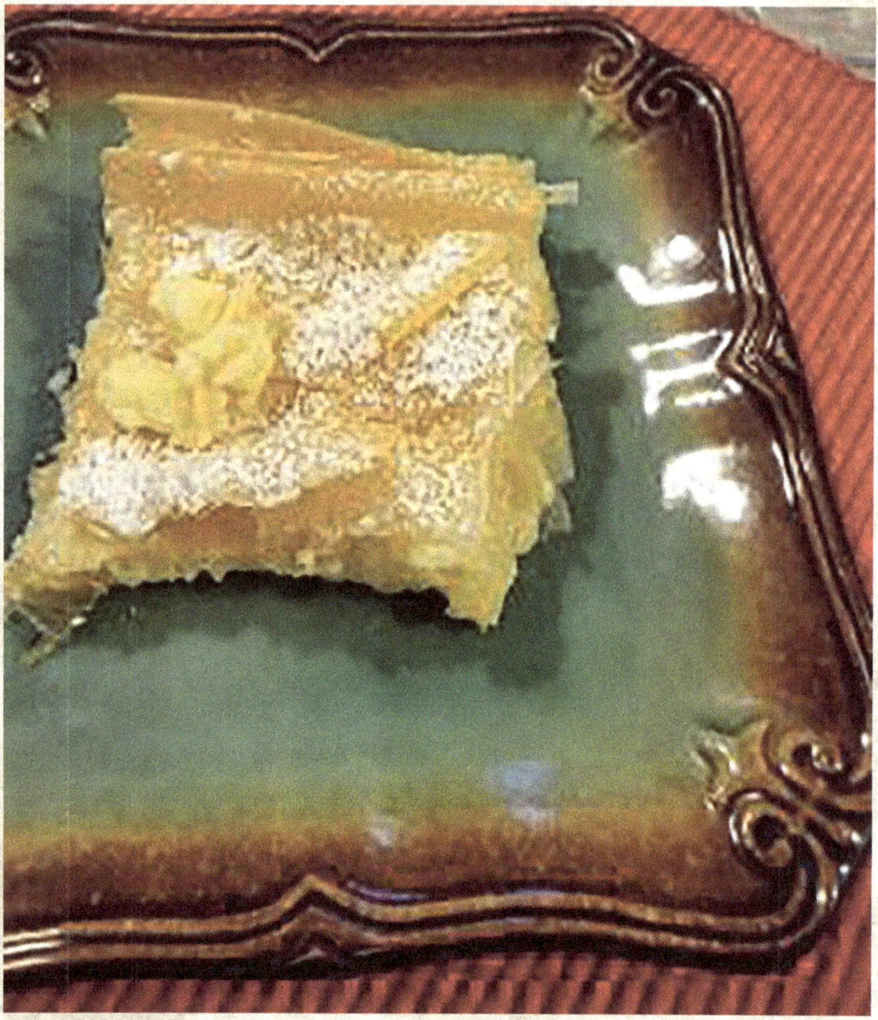

Result 2 kg

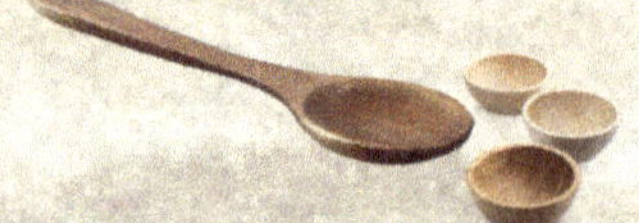

Milk *1.3kg*
Flour *250g*
Vanilla baton .... *½*
sugar *450g*
eggs .... *10 each*

Preparation: *Boil the milk with the vanilla seeds in a sauce pan.*

Separate the yolks from the eggs whites. Mix the yolks with the ¾ of the sugar quantity and the flour. Pour the hot milk over the yolk mixture, while continuously whisking for a homogenous result. Put the mixture back on the stove and continue whisking, until it thickens. Beat the eggs whites with the remaining sugar quantity until it forms hard peaks.

Fold the beaten eggs whites into the cooled composition. Serve as needed.

PECANS CRÈME

Result 2 kg

Pecans halved	700g
Milk	500ml
Eggs	5 each
Cinnamon	15g
bread crumbs	300g
sugar	500g
lemon zest	25g
vanillin	1/2g

Preparation: *Scald the bread crumbs with the hot milk. Mix it with the grounded pecans, eggs, and sugar. Mix it well until the composition is homogenous. Add the vanillin, cinnamon and lemon zest.*

GANESH CRÈME CHOCOLATE

Chocolate (dark) 900g
Heavy crème 700g
Vanillin.. 1/4g
sugar 500g
rom.. 100ml

Preparation: *Mix the chocolate (cut in small pieces) with the sugar and heavy cream. Set it on the stove ar reduced heat while continuously whisking, until the chocolate is melted. Get the composition out of the stove, and set the pan in a vase with iced water to cool off. Beat the composition until foams. Add the vanillin and rom.*

Note: the crème Ganesh can also be prepared as follows: boil the heavy cream and sugar. Take the pan out of the stove and the chocolate cubs. Set the pan on a vase with iced water, and then whisk it until foams. Add the rom and vanillin.

CHOCOLATE SAUCE

Sugar.. 800g
Eggs .... 5 each
Rom.. 50ml
milk 350ml
cacao 100g
vanillin.. 1/8g

Preparation: *beat the eggs with the sugar and thin it with milk. Add the cacao and mix well.*

Set it on the stove and boil it for 10 minutes after it started to boil. Let it cool off and add the rom and the vanillin.

CHEESE FOR THE PATISSERIES

Feta cheese.. 900g
Eggs .... 2 each
flour 100g

Preparation: *wash the feta cheese, and then ground it. Mix it with the eggs and sieved flour until homogenous.*

MEAT FOR THE PATISSERIES

Beef meat..425g
Onions 300g
Lard 20g
White bread...200g
eggs..4 each
pork meat...425g
pepper..2g

Preparation: *Cut the meat in cubs, clean the onions, wash and slice them. Put the onions in a pan with the lard to soften, and then add the meat.*

Introduce the pan in the oven until browns.

Let it cool off and ground them together with the moist white bread. Add the eggs, the salt and the pepper and mix well.

CHARLOTTE SAINT HONOREE

Result 10 portions

Milk	225ml
Eggs	2 each
Rom	50ml
Whipped cream	700g
sugar	250g
gelatin	20g
vanillin	1/10g
candied fruits	100g

Preparation: *beat the eggs with the sugar and thin it with the milk. Put the composition on the stove and bring it to a boil, whisking continuously. Take the pan off the stove and mix it with the gelatin that was dissolved in cold water until dissolved.*

Add the rom and the vanillin over the candied fruits that were cut in small cubs. After the composition is cooled off add the macerated fruits.

WHITE FONDANT

Sugar.. 10kg
Glucose 1kg
water 5l

Preparation: dissolve the sugar into the water and set it on stove to boil. The composition is ready when it forms large bubbles and it is probed by dropping few drops on a plate with cold water. If it forms like a candy, then is ready. Let is cool off, then swirl it with a wooden spoon until it changes the color to white.

You can mix it with cacao, or coffee, for a chocolate, or coffee fondant.

CARAMEL SUGAR

Result 1kg

Sugar.. 900g
water 100g

Preparation: put the sugar in a special pan for burning the sugar, set it on the stove and mix it continuous with a wooded pallet until the sugar is caramelized (when the sugar forms small air bubbles at the surface and the color change to brown, or dark brown). At this point add the water and continue boiling until the drops set on a piece of paper are dark brown and the consistency of candies.

Chapter III: Candied fruits

The candied fruits are sugary products that are obtained from fruits or parts of the fruits saturated with syrup from sugar and glucose.

Use glucose in proportion of 30% in rapport to the weight of the final product for the preparation of the syrup.

If the candied fruits are taken out of the syrup and set on a grate to dry off, it forms a layer of crystalized glucose at the surface.

The packing of the candied fruits is to be made in card board boxes, wooden boxes or sealed glass jars.

Keep them in a dry clean place, well ventilated, with temperature at 18 degrees Celsius and 75% humidity. Don't keep them in the sun.

CANDIED ORANGE PEELS

Result 2.2kg candied orange peels and 500g syrup

Orange peels.. *1.350kg*
Sugar.. *1.5kg*
glucose *660g*

Preparation: *separate the orange peels in 4 equal segments, then carefully peel them from the fruit. Soak the orange peels in cold water for at least 48 hours, and then boil them until soften.*

Take the peels out of the stove and place them in vases with cold water, changing the water few times.

Prepare the syrup as follows: 1/3 of the sugar quantity with double the water quantity and boil it until if forms a thin syrup.

Pour the cold syrup over the orange peels that were taken out of the water and arranged in form of spirals in a vase.

Measure the remaining sugar and portion it in 4 quantities,

The second day, mix the syrup from the orange peels, add ¼ of the sugar quantity, and boil it again with the orange peels. Pour it again in the vase and let it rest until the next day when you repeat the operation using the second ¼ of the sugar.

Repeat the operation on the 3rd sand 4th day.

On the 5th and 6th day use the glucose and repeat the same process.

On the 7th day, bring the syrup to a boil until it thickens then add the fruits and bring it to a boil again.

The 8th day, take the fruits out of the syrup and place them on a grill to dry off. Boil the syrup one more time.

Place the fruits in sealed jars, and pout the hot syrup on top of them. Let it cool and seal the jars.

CANDIED LEMON PEELS

Result 3.1 kg candied lemons and 2.7kg syrup

    Lemon peels 3.37kg
    Sugar.. 4kg
    glucose 1kg
    liquid color.. 10g

Preparation: *it is the same as for the candied orange peels with the difference that the lemons are shaved of the yellow part first (the lemon zest), and the first boiling water is thrown away and replaced with clean water.*

CANDIED CHERRIES

Result 18.5 kg candied cherries and 12kg syrop

    Cherries (with pits).. 50kg
    Cherries (without pits) .... 32 kg
    sugar 20kg
    glucose 4kg

Preparation: *wash and core the cherries. The rest of the preparation is the same as for the candied orange peels.*

CANDIED WATERMELON

Raw water melon	315kg
Clean water melon	118kg
Sugar	20kg
glucose	17kg
color	25g

Preparation: *before boiling, first, peel the green part off and the center part, and put the water melon peels in a basin with salt water prepared as such: 250g salt to 1ol water, and keep it there for 4 days. Then take them out and put them in a vase with cold water that needs to be changed for 3 days.*

The rest is the same as for candied orange peels.

CANDIED PEARS

Pears	56kg
Sugar	20kg
glucose	6kg
color	25g

Preparation: *scald the pears in boiled water, and then peel them in a thin, uniform layer. As you peel them, put them in a vase with water and meth bisulfite to remain white. Core the pears. Boil the pears until softened.*

Precede the same as for the other candied fruits (See above)

Chapter IV: Tender dough

It is called tender dough for it takes big quantities of butter, or lard for its preparation. The materials needed for the tender dough are: flour, eggs, sugar, milk, butter or lard, baking powder, and baking soda, and condiments.

This dough is not kneaded and has to be kept in the refrigerator, before using. Use powder sugar for these recipes.

CORABIOARE

Flour 2.8kg
Lard 1kg
Oil.. 150ml
Baking powder................................... 30g
powder sugar 1.1kg
vanillin... 1/4g
eggs... 3 each

Preparation: *Sieve the flour on a working surface. Make a hole in the middle of the flour and add ¾ of the sugar quantity and the eggs. Mix with your hands until the sugar crystals are dissolved. Add the lard, the baking powder, and the vanillin, and incorporate the flour until it forms dough. Cover the dough in plastic liner and put it in the fridge.*

Let it cool in the fridge for at least 20 minutes up to overnight.

Spread the dough in long rolls with 3cm-4cm in diameter, flatten the roll with hands and apply a motive with the fork's teeth on its entire length. Cut rhombs and place them on a try and bake them at a good heat, until browns. Serve them with powder sugar.

LINTZER WITH JAM

Flour	*1.4kg*
Butter	*500g*
Eggs	*10 each*
Vanillin	*1/4g*
Oil	*400g*
sugar	*500g*
baking powder	*20g*
lemon zest from	*1 to 2 lemons*
orange zest	*110g*
jam	*2kg*

Preparation: *for the tender dough preparation: beat the butter, oil and sugar until the sugar crystals dissolve; add the eggs, the baking powder, the condiments and the flour. Mix it all together until it forms dough and let it rest in the refrigerator for at least 20 minutes.*

Spread the ¾ of the dough in a 2cm to 3 cm thickness layer, and set it on a tray to half bake in the oven.

Spread jam over the bottom layer half-baked), and add the top layer (from the remaining dough) in strips (to form a grill).

Wash the top layer with a beaten egg. Bake it until golden brown.

FIGARO

Flour	1.8kg
Oil	750ml
Eggs (yolks 18)	9 each
sugar	480g
butter	250g
baking powder	30g

For the glaze

Pecans shelled	1kg
Eggs (whites 28)	14 each
sugar	1.450kg
flour	200g

Preparation: *Prepare the dough the same as for lintzer (see above). After cooling in the refrigerator for at least 20 minutes, spared the dough in a 2cm thick layer and place it on a tray. Half bake it in the oven. Take it out of the oven, and spread the jam over it.*

Pour on top the glaze that is prepared as such: mix the eggs whites with the grounded pecans and sugar on the stove until hot. Take it out of the stove and add the flour. Spread the glaze in a uniform layer in top of the jam.

Bake the pie at medium heat until golden brown. Cut it in pieces and serve it warm.

TARTE WITH PECANS

Flour 1.6kg
Butter.. 725g
Powder sugar 700g
Shelled pecans 900g
eggs... 16 each
sugar 900g
jam 500g
baking powder 25g

Preparation: *Prepare the tender dough the same as for Corabioare (see above).*

Introduce the filo dough (1/2 cm thickness) into the tart forms and bake them half way through. Take them out of the oven and place some jam inside the tarts, then pour in top the pecan glaze that is prepared the same as for the Figaro (see above). Put them back in the oven and bake those until the surface of the tarts are luscious.

TARTE WITH FRUITS

Flour	*2.2kg*
Oil	*500ml*
Eggs	*8 each*
Vanillin	*1/4g*
sugar	*450g*
butter	*300g*
milk	*500ml*
baking powder	*20g*

Vanilla crème

Milk	*1.2l*
Flour	*250g*
Fruits (strawberries, Raspberries, grapes)	*3kg*
eggs	*3 each*
sugar	*300g*
fruits jam	*1kg*

Preparation: *prepare the tarts the same was as for the tarts with pecans (see above) with the difference that the tarts are fully baked. Then, take them out of the forms, and fill them with vanilla crème, and set on top the washed and dried fruits. Cover the fruits entirely with the jam that was warmed up.*

SALTY BATON

Result 2.7 kg

Flour	2kg
Sugar	400g
Eggs	4 each
chimen	75g
butter	1kg
salt	50g
milk	200ml

Preparation: *Sieve the flour on the working surface. Make a hole in the middle of the flour mountain, and add the eggs, the salt, the chimen, and the sugar. Mix it until the sugar and salt crystals are dissolved. Add the butter and incorporate the flour to form dough. Put the dough in the refrigerator for at least 20 minutes. Then, roll out the batons about 1cm thickens and 8 cm length, wash them with egg, and set them on a tray in the oven. Bake them at a good heat.*

APPLE PIE

Flour	2.7kg
Baking powder	40g
Milk	1l
Apples	4kg
Cinnamon	20g
Vanillin	1g
butter	800g
eggs	15 each
bread crumbs	1.5kg
sugar	1.7kg
oil	800ml
powder sugar	300g

Preparation: *Sieve the flour on the working surface, to form a mountain. Make a hole in the middle of the mountain and add the eggs, the baking powder, the salt and 700g of sugar. Mix it until the sugar crystals are dissolved, then add the butter and continue to mix and incorporate the flour until it forms dough. Set the dough in the refrigerator for at least 20 minutes to up to 2 hours. Take it out, and cut it in 2, and spread two layers of 1cm thickness.*

Set one layer on the tray and pour the apples mixture on top.

Prepare the apple mixture as such: peel the apples and shred them. Boil them with the oil, the remaining sugar, grounded cinnamon, vanillin and bread crumbs until the water evaporates.

Set the second layer of dough on top of the apple mixture, wash it with egg and cut few holes or slits in it.

Bake it until golden brown. Serve it with powder sugar.

COTTAGE CHEESE AND RAISINS PIE

Flour .... 3 kg
Butter... 800g
Cottage cheese.. 3.3kg
Raisins 250g
Lemon zest 400g
Milk.. 1.5l
grits 500g
eggs .... 20 each
oil... 750ml
vanillin.. 1g
sugar 3kg
baking powder 50g

Preparation: *it is the same as for the apple pie (see above) with the difference that is made with cottage cheese that is prepared as such: mix the cottage cheese, with the grits, eggs, raisins, lemon zest, sugar, and vanillin.*

Chapter V: Leavened dough

SIMPLE DOUGHNUTS

Result 100 pieces of 60g each

Flour	3.6kg
Leaven	150g
Milk	1l
Sugar	500g
Vanillin	1/4g
oil	900ml
powder sugar	150g
eggs	5 each
salt	50g

Preparation: *prepare the dough as in Semi-fabricates-Savarin. Let it to leaven. Take it out of the bowl and form a roll, cut it in pieces and form it in balls. Set the balls on the working surface; wash their surface with oil and let then leaven.*

Heat up the oil and put the doughnuts I hot oil with the face that was sitting on the working surface, first. Turned them around and take them out of the oil when golden brown. Let them cool off, and powder them with a little flour to absorb the grease, and then serve them with powder sugar.

DOUGHNUTS FILLED WITH JAM

Flour 3.4kg
Milk 1.5l
Leaven 200g
Butter for the dough 200g
Oil for boiling 800g
Eggs .... 8 each
sugar 300g
powder sugar 200g
jam 700g
vanillin 1/4g
salt 50g

Preparation: *prepare them the same as the simple doughnuts, with the difference that before powdering them, make a hole at one end with a stick and fill it with jam using a squeezing bag with a metallic end.*

SIMPLE ROLLS

Flour 3.4kg
Milk..1l
Leaven 200g
Sugar...650g
vanillin..1/4g
salt..50g
oil...200ml
eggs...7 each

Preparation: *prepare the dough as for the sweet bread, roll it in along roll and cut it in pieces.*

Form each piece in for of a triangle. Roll the triangle starting from the base and curve them like an elbow. Put them on tray coated with oil. Let them rise, wash them with egg, and add a little sugar in the middle of each piece for decorum. Bake them at medium heat, then at a good heat.

ROLLS FILLED WITH JAM

Flour	3.4kg
Leaven	200g
Milk	1l
Eggs	7 each
Sugar	400g
jam	1.75kg
vanillin	1/4g
salt	50g
oil	200ml

Preparation: *it is the same as for the simple rolls with the difference that they are filled with jam instead of sugar.*

ROLLS FILLED WITH PECANS

Result 100 pieces of 60g each

Flour 3.4kg
Milk.. 1l
Sugar... 400g
Eggs .... each
Salt.. 50g
Oil.. 200g

for the pecans cream

pecans 400g
sugar 350g
vanillin... 1/4g

Preparation: it is the same as for the simple rolls with the difference that before rolling add the pecans cream in the middle.

BRANZOAICE

Flour	3.4 kg
Sugar	800g
Oil	400g
Eggs	5 each
Leaven	200g
salt	50g
cheese (ricotta)	600g
grits	350g
eggs for washing	4 each

Preparation: prepare the leavened dough as for the sweet bread recipe, then stretch it in a long roll and cut it in pieces. Round the pieces in balls and set them in a tray that was covered with oil.

Dig a hole in the middle of each piece and add the cheese mixture as prepared in chapter semi- fabricate. Let them rise, wash them with eggs, and bake them first at medium heat then at a good heat.

BANZOAICE MOLDOVENESTI

Result 100 pieces of 90g each

Flour *3.9kg*
Sugar *1.5kg*
Oil *200g*
Eggs .... *3 each*
Grits *50g*
cottage cheese *3kg*
leaven *375g*
vanillin *1/2g*
salt *100g*

Preparation: *Prepare the leavened dough as for sweet bread, let it rise, form a long roll and cut it in pieces. Roll them in balls. Let it rest. Spread each ball it in a square form. Add the cheese mixture as prepared in semi-fabricate chapter, close the four corners of the square (2 at a time) to form an envelope. Set them in a tray covered with oil at a medium heat first, then at a good heat. Serve them with powder sugar.*

SAVARIN

Result 100 pieces of 120g each

Flour .... 2.5 kg
Leaven 150g
Milk 2l
Sugar 200g
Oil 300ml
Salt 50g
Eggs .... 9 each
Lemon zest from 1/2lemons

For syrup

Sugar 2.8kg
water 4l
rom essence 10ml

for finish

whipped cream 2.1kg
sugar 200g
vanillin 1/4g
jam 500g

Preparation: *prepare the leavened dough as presented in the chapter semi-fabricate. After they are cold, dunk them in syrup until moist. Set them on a grate, cut a lid and glaze the lid with jam.*

Fill them with whipped cream inside.

BRAIDED SWEET BREAD

Result 100 pieces of 60g each

Flour .... *3.4 kg*
Leaven *200g*
Oil.. *200ml*
Sugar... *650g*
milk.. *1l*
vanillin.. *1/4g*
salt... *50g*
eggs... *7 each*

Preparation: *Prepare the leavened dough as for the sweet bread. Roll it in a long wick and cut it in pieces. Then roll each piece it in a thin wick of 1cm in diameter. Cut it in 2 and start braiding 4 thin wicks. Set the bread into the tray; make sure the ends are turned down. Let it rise. Wash it with egg and bake it at medium heat.*

TENDER BATONS

Result 100 pieces of 40g each

Flour 3kg
Leaven 150g
Oil.. 140ml
Salt... 100g
chimen 25g
sugar 125g
eggs.. 3 each
water

Preparation: *prepare the leavened dough and add the chime.*

After it rose, roll in in forms of batons app. 25cm-30cm long. Set them on a tray coated with oil and let them rise. Wash them with egg wash and bale them at a medium heat.

MELCI (SNAILS)

Flour 3.4kg
Leaven 200g
Eggs .... 7 each
Sugar.. 350g
Oil... 250ml
Milk.. 1.1l
Salt... 100g
Lemon peel from .... ½ lemon
Vanillin... 1/4g

for the pecan cream

pecans shelled 1kg
sugar 400g
bread crumbs 500g
lemon zest... 1/4g
cinnamon powder 5g

for syrup

sugar 2kg
glucose 250g
Vanillin.. 1/4g
Rom essence 5g

Preparation: *Prepare the leavened dough (see the semi-fabricates chapter). Spread a sheet of 1cm thickness. Smear it with the pecans cream (see the semi-fabricates chapter). Roll it and cut it in pieces of 3 cm width. Set it with the cut side up in a tray and let it rise. Wash them with the egg wash and bake them. Pour the cold syrup over the not pastries.*

POLISH PRETZELS

Flour 3.3kg
Milk.. 1.5l
Leaven 180g
Sugar.. 400g
Oil.. 200ml

For syrup

Sugar.. 2.4kg
Glucose 300g
Rom essence 10ml
Vanillin.. 1/4g
butter 550g
lemon .... 1 each
vanillin.. 1/2g
eggs.. 15 each
salt... 50g

Preparation: *Prepare the leavened dough. Let it rise, and spread a sheet of 1cm thickness. Spread the butter over the entire sheet and fold it in 4, then set it in the refrigerator for at least 20 minutes. Spread it again, and cut it in strips of 3cm wide and 25cm long. Twist both ends of the strips in opposite directions and give it the form of 8. Set them up in the tray and let it rise.*

Wash them with the egg wash and bake them first at medium heat them at a good heat until golden brown. Dunk the hot pretzels in cold syrup, one by one.

BRIOCHE

Result 100 pieces of 60g each

Flour 3.5kg
Eggs 10each
Oil.. 400ml
Sugar.. 1kg
Leaven 150g
salt... 50g
baking powder 40g
lemon zest.. 100g
water 1.5l

Preparation: prepare the leavened dough and add to it also the baking powder beside the leaven to make the dough softer. Set the dough in forms coated with oil, same as for the savarin, and bake them first at medium heat, then at a good heat. When ready they should have a crest on top.

SWEET BREAD (COZONAC SIMPLU)

Result 7.5kg

Flour	4.5kg
Milk	1.5l
Sugar	1.35kg
Eggs (20yolk)	10each
Leaven	500g
Vanillin	1/2g
Lemon zest	100g
salt	50g
lard	250g
oil	650g
eggs for wash	2 each
sugar for the forms	280g
butter for forms	200g

Preparation:

1. *Prepare the miaua as such: mix the leaven with warm milk and sugar and thicken it with flour, then cover it with flour and let it rise.*

2. *Prepare the shadou as such: mix the eggs with the salt, the sugar, and vanillin and lemon zest and beat it until the sugar crystals are all dissolved.*

3. *Pour the maiaua into the flour and add the shadou and incorporate the flour and knead the dough until it unglues from hands and vase's walls.*

4. *Add the lard and oil and knead by overlapping the dough.*

5. *Let it rise*

6. *Cover the forms with butter and granulated sugar.*

7. *After the dough has rose, set it in forms by braiding it.*

8. *Let it rise again*

9. *Wash it with the egg wash*

10. *Set in in oven at a reduced heat first, then at medium heat.*

SWEET BREAD WITH PECANS

Result 5.250kg

Flour 2kg
Milk.. 599ml
Sugar... 400g
Leaven 150g
Eggs .... 12 each
Vanillin.. ½ baton
Lemon .... 1 each
Salt... 50g
Oil... 300ml
Eggs for egg wash.................................... 2 each

for the pecans cream

pecans halved 3kg
milk... 500ml
sugar 700g
bread crumbs.. 300g
cinnamon 5g
rom essence 5ml
raisins.. 50g
lemon zest... ½ lemons

Preparation: *Prepare the dough the same as for the simple sweet bread (see above). Spread it in a sheet of 1.5 cm thickness and spread it with the pecans cream (see the semi-fabricate chapter). Roll it and set it in forms or on a tray coated with oil. Let it rise. Wash it with egg wash and bake it first at a reduced heat, then a medium heat.*

SWEET BREAD WITH RAISINS.

Flour	4kg
Milk	1l
Leaven	250g
Sugar	1kg
Eggs	16 each
Butter	200g
Sugar for forms	300g
oil	750ml
salt	50g
vanillin	1/2baton
lemon zest	from 1 lemon
raisins	100g
rom essence	5g

Preparation: *it is the same as for the simple sweet bread with the difference that there are added raisins.*

Chapter VI: Pie dough

Its name pie dough as it stretches thin as a sheet of paper

The materials used for the pie dough are: flour, salt, water, lard. For a good pie, the materials need to be the first quality.

Preparation: sieve the flour on the working surface, or a vase. Make a hole in the middle of the flour mountain and add the salt and the water. Mix it until the salt crystals are dissolved.

Incorporate the flour and knead it until it forms dough of hard consistence. Let it rest to recoup its elasticity.

Knead it again and form a long roll (wick). Cut it in pieces and round each piece perfectly. Coat them with lard and let them rest to recoup their elasticity.

Place each piece on the working surface that was coated with lard, thin it using a rolling pin and rotate it around in the air. Palpate the sheet with lard and fold it as needed.

FETA CHEESE PIE

Flour	800g
Lard	200g
Grits	100g
cheese (feta)	800g
eggs	2 each
salt	50g

Preparation: sieve the four on the working surface. Dissolve the salt into the water and incorporate the flour to obtain dough of hard consistency.

Let it rest. Form a wick and cut it in 4 pieces, two large and two small. Round each piece perfectly and smear them with lard. Let them rest.

Stretch the smaller balls, grease them and put them one in top of the other.

When the dough got its elasticity spread one of the larger balls in a thin sheet. Grease it and fold it in 3 to form the base of the pie.

Spread the second large ball, and grease it, then add the cheese mixture at one end (see the semi- fabricate chapter) then fold it to form a round form.

The two smaller balls form the face of the pie. Spread the dough and grease it and add the cheese mixture to one end. Give it a round form. Tack to edges under, grease the surface and set it in around form. Bake it until its volume increases and the color is golden brown.

MEAT PIE

Flour	750g
Onions	2kg
Lard	200g
Pepper	5g
beef meat	750g
white bread	200g
oil	50ml
salt	90g

Preparation: *it is the same as for the feta cheese pie with the difference that the filling is meat filing (see the preparation in the semi-fabricate chapter).*

COTTAGE CHEESE PIE

Flour	3.6kg
Salt	100g
Eggs	12 each
Raisins	100g
lard	800g
cottage cheese	4kg
sugar	1.4kg
lemon zest	120g

Preparation: *it is the same as for the cheese pie with the difference that the filling is prepared as such: mix the cottage cheese with the flour, eggs, sugar and lemon zest, then add the raisins.*

MERDENELE WITH MEAT

Flour 3.3kg
Lard 1.5kg
Eggs .... 10 each
Meat (boneless)...................................... 2kg
onions 4kg
pepper... 10g
oil... 150ml
salt... 50g

Preparation: *prepare the pie dough, roll it in wick and cut pieces, then roll the pieces into balls. Grease the balls. Let them rest. Spread each ball with the rolling pin in a square sheet. Grease the surface of each sheet and fold it in 3 width wise and in 4 length wise. Put it in the refrigerator until the lard solidifies. Spread each sheet with the rolling pin, or the palm of your hand, in a square form. Grease it and fold the two opposite corners, then add the meat filling (see the semi- fabricate chapter for the meat filling) and close the other two corners. Grease them, and set them on a tray and bake them at a good heat.*

MERDENELE WITH CHEESE

Result 100 pieces of 100g each

    Flour *3.3kg*
    Cheese *1.9kg*
    Grits *200g*
    lard *1.5kg*
    salt *50g*
    eggs .... *6 each*

Preparation: *it is the same as for the merdenele with meat with the difference that the filling is cheese mix instead of meat.*

The cheese mix is prepared as such: ground the cheese (feta), and mix it with the eggs and the cooked and cooled grits.

SPINACH PIE

Flour 800g
Lard 200g
Spinach.. 1.1 kg
Eggs .... 2 each
pepper.. 2g
parmesan cheese.................................... 200g
oil... 50ml
salt... 50g

Preparation: *it is the same as for the cheese pie with the difference that the cheese filling is replaced with the spinach filling that is prepared as such:*

Wash the spinach and scald it in boiling water and salt. Let it cool off and cut it in small pieces. Cook it in a pan with hot oil, then and add the salt, pepper, and grated parmesan cheese.

CABBAGE PIE

Flour 750g
Lard 250g
Cabbage 2.5kg
pepper.. 20g
salt... 50g

Preparation: *it is the same as for the cheese pie with the difference that the filling is prepared as such: wash the cabbage and remove exterior leaves and the core. Cut it in thin slices and knead it with salt and let it rest for 30 minutes, after that drain the water. Cook the cabbage in lard and add salt and pepper as needed.*

Chapter VII: Greek filo

For the preparation of the Greek filo there are needed the following materials: flour, corn starch, salt, water and oil. For the best results all primary materials need to be the first quality.

Preparation: *sieve the flour on the working surface. Make a hole in the middle of the flour mountain and add the water the salt and the oil.*

Mix it until the salt is dissolved. Incorporate the flour and knead to form homogenous dough.

Pound the dough against the working surface (wooden board) until it forms air boules. Cut it in pieces, round each piece perfectly, grease them with oil, and let it rest.

Start stretching the dough, first with the rolling pin then with your hands from the middle toward the edges, preferable on a table cloth was covered with flour until very thin. Let it dry. Cut the thick edges and cut the sheet in rectangular sheets. Set the sheets one on top of the other with corn starch sprinkled between the sheets. Roll them and pack them in paper.

APPLE STRUDEL

Greek filo	350g
Butter	100g

For the filling

Apples	1kg
sugar	130g
powder sugar	20g

Preparation: *set the Greek fillos one by one in a tray, or working surface first, sprinkle each filo with melted butter (approx. 8 to 10 sheets per roll), add the filling at one end, and roll, making sure you tack the edges as you roll.*

Brush melted butter on top of each roll. Set the rolls in a try that was buttered and bake them at medium heat. Cut it in pieces and serve them with powder sugar.

The filling for the strudel can also be cottage cheese with raisins, or pecans cream (see the semi- fabricate section)

STRUDEL WITH CHERRIES

Four...500g
Oil..20ml
Salt...10g
Butter...200g
cherries...1kg
sugar..300g
bread crumbs..100g

Preparation: *prepare the Greek fillos described above. Set them one in top of the other with melted butter sprinkled between each sheet (about 8 to 10 sheets per roll), set the filling at one end (on the long side of the sheets) and roll them in form of a cylinder. Brush each roll with melted butter, set them in a tray that was buttered and bake them at a medium heat until golden brown. Cut the rolls in pieces and serve them with powdered sugar.*

STRUDEL WITH COTTAGE CHEESE

Flour 500g
Oil..20ml
Salt...10g
Butter...200g
Cottage cheese...1kg
eggs...2 each
sugar 150g
flour (bread crumbs)....................................100g
lemon zest...10g
raisins...25g

Preparation: *it is the same as for the strudel with apple with the difference that the filling is cottage cheese with raisins (see the semi-fabricate chapter).*

BAKLAVA

Result 100 pieces of 100g each

Greek fillos	3.5 kg
Oil	550ml
Pecans halved	2kg
Butter	500g
Sugar	3 kg
glucose	750g
rose water	100g
vanillin	1/2g
lemon zest	20g

Preparation: *Divide the fillos in 3 parts and the filling in 2 portions.*

Set on third of the Greek fillos on a tray, each fillo sprinkled with melted butter, then set one portion of the grounded pecans on top of it. Set the second layer of fillos, then the second part of the grounded pecans, and finally the last of the fillos. Grease the surface with melted butter and let it in refrigerator for 30 minutes. Cut it in square pieces and bake it until golden brown. Pour cold syrup over the hot baklava.

SARAILIE

Greek fillos	1.5kg
Oil	550g
Pecans halved	2kg
Butter	500g
Lemon zest	20g
sugar	3kg
glucose	750g
rose water	100ml
vanillin	1/2g

Preparation: place 2 fillos of about 30 to 40cm, each sprinkled with oil, one in top of the other. Add the pecans. Turn in the edges and roll it on a stick of 1.5cm diameter. Push ends toward the center, like a harmonic, then take it out of the stick, cut it in 2 and place it on a greased tray, one next to the other to keep the form. Grease the surface of the rolls, and bake them until golden brown. Pour cold syrup over them when hot from the oven.

TRIGONES WITH PECAN CREAM

Greek fillos 3kg
Oil... 550ml
Butter... 450g
Pecans cream 3kg
Lemon zest 30g
sugar 2.5kg
glucose 500g
fistic essence... 10g
vanillin... 1/2g

Preparation: take 2 Greek fillos 15x40cm, each sprinkled with oil, set them one in top of the other, turn in the edges on both ends to for a rectangle of 10x12cm. Place the pecan cream filling on one end (about 40 g each) and start folding from the end with the filling to form a triangle, then fold again to form the second triangle. Grease the surface and bake them until golden brown. Dunk each triangle in cold syrup (after piercing the sides).

Chapter VIII: Scalded dough

It's called scalded dough because it is necessary to scald the flour. The prime materials for the scalded dough are: flour, lard, eggs and water.

Preparation: *in a pan put the water and grease to boil. When it starts boiling, add the flour in block. Mix it well and quick to form an homogenous dough (without lumps). Take out of the stove and add the eggs, one by one. Set it in forms, as needed, using a bag with a tip.*

The scalded dough it is used for: eclairs, profiterole, choux a la crème, Saint Honoree.

CHOCOLATE ÉCLAIR

Result 100 pieces of 100g each

Eclairs	100 pieces
Cacao	100g
Fondant	3kg
vanilla crème	6kg
rom	200ml

Preparation: *pour the scalded dough with the bag in forms of batons. Bake them first at a good heat for 10 minutes, without opening the oven, then reduce the heat. They are ready when their volume increases and the color is golden brown and are detached from the tray. Cut them at one end and fill them with vanilla crème (see the semi-fabricate chapter) with rom. Glaze them with chocolate fondant. To obtain a luscious surface, brush syrup on top of the eclairs prior to applying the fondant.*

CHOUX A LA CRÈME

Result 25 pieces of 110g each

Choux	25 each
Vanilla crème	1.4kg
Candied oranges	250g
rom	50ml
wiped cream	1.1kg
powder sugar	50g

Preparation: *pour the dough on the trays in a round form using a bag. Bake them the same as for the eclairs. Let them cool off. Cut a lid for each choux and fill in the vanilla crème that was mixed with rom. Add a dollop of wiped cream mixed with the cubed candied oranges in top and set the lid back. Powder the lid with powdered sugar.*

SALAMBO

Salambo shells .... 45 each
Vanilla crème 500g
choux .... 45 each
sugar for glaze 500g

Preparation: *pour the scalded dough composition using the bag in round forms on a tray in groups of 3 such that after baking the group of 3 will stick together. Separately bake a small choux for each group of 3 salambo. Fill the salambo and the choux with vanilla crème and glaze them with caramel sugar. Place one small choux in top of the salambo trio group.*

PROFITEROLE WITH CHOCOLATE SAUCE

Profiterole shells 600g
Wiped cream 1kg
vanilla crème 800g
chocolate sauce 300g

Preparation: *the preparation is the same as for the profiteroles with ice cream with the difference that it is served simple ornate with wiped cream and chocolate sauce (see semi-fabricate chapter).*

PROFITEROLE WITH ICE CREAM

Result 10 portions of 250g each

Profiterole shells 600g
Vanilla cream.. 800g
Chocolate sauce 300g
ice cream 600g
wiped cream... 600g

Preparation: *pour the scalded dough composition (using a bag) in round forms (the size of a pecan). Bake them and fill them with vanilla cream.*

Serve the ice cream surrounded by the profiteroles and topped with wiped cream and chocolate sauce.

Chapter IX

FEUILLETAGE (FRENCH DOUGH)

For the French dough are used the following prime materials:

Flour 1.250kg
Butter... 1kg
Vinegar 10ml
salt.. 50g
water 500ml

For this recipe are used equal quantities of flour and butter. The rest of the flour is used for folding.

Preparation: *prepare medium consistency dough from ¾ of the flour quantity, salt, water and vinegar. Knead it well until is detaching from the hands and the working surface. Round it in a ball, crest it, and let it rest.*

Spread the hardened butter on the working surface with the rolling pin, to eliminate the excess water, mix it quick with the remaining flour, fold it, and put it in the refrigerator.

Spread the dough on the working surface in form of a rhomb. Add the cold butter and turn the edges of the dough to cover the butter entirely. Spread it with the rolling pin from middle to edges and both sides of the dough to obtain a rectangle of 2 – 3 cm thickness. Fold it in four and let it rest in the refrigerator. Repeat the operation 3 more times. After the last cooling it is used as needed.

PARMESAN BATONS

    French dough *2.6kg*
    Flour *100g*
    parmesan *0.3kg*
    eggs .... *2 each*

Preparation: *prepare the French dough and spread it in a thin sheet of 1/2cm thickness.*

Brush the surface with beaten eggs and shred the parmesan cheese on top. Cut, with a hot knife, in long pieces of 3cm width, and set them on a tray that was sprinkled with water. Bake then first at a good heat, then at medium heat. Serve them with consommé.

BATONS WITH SESAME

Result 1 kg

French dough 1.250kg
Sugar 50g
Sesame 50g
flour for folding 50g
egg for washing 1each

Preparation: spread a sheet of ½ cm thickness. Wash it with the beaten egg and sprinkle sesame on top. Cut the sheet in long strips of 8-10cm and 3 cm wide. Set them on a tray in spirals or straight and bake then first at a good heat, then at medium heat.

VOL-AU-VENT

Flour 1.2kg
Butter... 1kg
Vinegar 9degrees 10ml
salt.. 50g
eggs for washing................................. 2 each

Preparation: prepare the French dough. Stretch it in a sheet of 1/2cm thickness. Cut half of it in round circles with a diameter of 8-10cm, and the other half cut in circles with diameter of 4-5cm.

Wash both pieces with egg wash and set them one in top of the other (circles with the whole in top of the solid circles), and wash the top circle with the egg wash. Set them on a tray and bake them first at a good heat, then at medium heat. On a separate tray bake the lids (the 4-5cm circles).

Serve them filled with mushroom sauté, or chicken sauté, or pea's sauté. Add the lids on top and grease them with butter.

PATE WITH CHEESE

Butter	2.2kg
Flour	2.8kg
Vinegar	20ml
Salt	50g
cottage cheese	1kg
feta cheese	500g
eggs	4 each

Preparation: prepare the French dough. Spread a sheet on 1/3cm thick. Cut it in rectangular forms. Wash it with egg on one side. Set the filling in the middle and fold the edges in to form a rectangle. Wash them with the beaten eggs and bake them at a good heat first, then at medium heat.

PATE WITH MEAT

Butter..2.1kg
Flour 2.8kg
Vinegar 20ml
Salt...50g
Ground beef 1.3kg
onions 1kg
eggs...4 each
pepper..1g
lard..100g

Preparation: prepare the same way as the pate with cheese (above) with the difference that the filling is meat instead of cheese (see the semi-fabricate chapter for filling) and the form is round.

ROLLS WITH APPLES (CORNULETE)

Flour	1.9kg
Butter	1.5 kg
Apples	8kg
Cinnamon	50g
Salt	50g
vinegar	20g
sugar	900g
bread crumbs	300g
powder sugar	200g

Preparation: spread the French dough in a sheet of 1.5cm thickness. Set the apple filling on one end after sprinkling the bread crumbs. Roll it until the ends meet to form a cylinder of 3cm in diameter. Cut in in pieces of 12cm long. Set them in a tray in form of an elbow. Bake them first at a good heat, then at medium heat. Serve them with powder sugar.

BUSHEL WITH PECANS

Flour 1.8kg
Butter.. 1.5kg
Salt... 50g
Vinegar 20ml
Sugar.. 1.6kg
Glucose 200g
pecans halved 700g
lemon zest.. ½ lemon
vanillin.. 1/4g
rom essence 10ml
bread crumbs 60g

Preparation: *spread the French dough in a sheet of ½ cm. Pecan cream is poured on one end with the posh with dui, on the length of the sheet. Roll it until the ends meet and cut the edges. Precede the same until all dough and filling is finished. Wash it with egg wash and print a décor with the fork's teeth for the entire length. Cut it in pieces of 4–5cm length. Sprinkle the tray with water and set the bushels. After baking pour cold syrup over them.*

APPLE STRUDEL

French dough (raw)	*5kg*
Apples	*18kg*
Sugar	*2.5kg*
Bread crumbs	*1kg*
Eggs	*2 each*
cinnamon	*50g*
vanillin	*1g*
flour for folding	*200g*
powder sugar	*200g*

Preparation: *spread the French dough in a sheet of 1cm thickness. Sprinkle the bread crumbs. Add the apple filling at one end to form a cylinder of 5-6cm in diameter. Roll it until the edged meet. Wash them with egg wash. It can be decorated with dough strips and forms, cut with the dui. Bake it first at a good heat then at medium heat. When cooled off cut it in rhombs and powder then with powder sugar.*

BAKLAVA

Result 110 pieces of 115 g each

Flour	*2.6kg*
Butter	*1.6kg*
Flour for the butter	*200g*
Flour for the folding	*200g*
Salt	*60g*
Vinegar 9 degrees	*20ml*
Pecans halved	*2.7kg*
cinnamon	*20g*
glucose	*1.4kg*
vanillin	*1/2g*
fistic essence	*6g*
lemon zest	*20g*
butter for grease	*200g*
sugar	*6.45 kg*

Preparation: *prepare the French dough that is folded only 2 times in four. Ensemble as such:*

20% of the dough set in on the tray. Spread half of the pecans quantity that were grounded and mixed with cinnamon, then the other 20% of the French dough and again spread the grounded pecans mixed with cinnamon. The remaining 60 % of the French dough is spread on top and greased with melted butter. Let the butter harden then cut the baklava in rhomb pieces. Push a whole clove in the middle of each piece Bake it until golden brown and then pout the col syrup in top of the hot baklava.

COTTAGE CHEESE PIE

Result 100 pieces of 160g each

French dough (raw)	6kg
Cottage cheese	7kg
Flour	1kg
Sugar	1.8kg
Vanillin	2g
eggs	40 each
raisins	1kg
lemon zest	200g
flour for folding	250g

Preparation: spread the French dough in a sheet of 1/2cm thickness. Cut it at the tray dimension and set it in the tray that was sprinkled with water. Set the filling (see the semi-fabricate section).

Set the second sheet in top of the filling and wash it with egg wash. Close the edges and imprint a décor with the fork's teeth. Bake first at a good heat, then at medium heat until golden brown.

Cut it when cold.

MEAT PIE

French dough (raw)......................................1.1 kg
Pork meat...600g
Onions 300g
Bread crumbs...100g
Salt..20g
pepper..1/2g
eggs..3 each
2 eggs for filling
1 egg for wash

Preparation: *it is the same as for the cottage cheese pie with the only difference that the filling is meat instead of cheese (see the semi-fabricate section).*

APPLE PIE

Result 110 pieces of 130g

French dough (raw)..................................9kg
Apples 18kg
Sugar..................................2.5kg
Bread crumbs..................................1kg
Eggs ....4 each
cinnamon 15g
flour 200g
vanillin..................................1g
glucose 200g

Preparation: *it is the dame as for the cottage cheese pie with the difference that once it is out of the oven, brush its surface with glucose to be luscious.*

PIE WITH CHERRIES

Result 100 pieces of 120g each

French dough (raw)..*5kg*
Cherries...*15kg*
Sugar..*2.7kg*
Bread crumbs..*1kg*
flour *200g*
vanillin..*1g*
powder sugar *200g*

Preparation: *preparation it is the same as for the cheese pie with the difference that the filling is cherries instead of cheese. After cooling, cut it in pieces and powder with powder sugar.*

The cherries' filling is prepared as follows: wash and pit out the cherries, mix it with the sugar, vanillin and a portion of the bread crumbs. The rest of the bread crumbs are spread over the dough sheet before applying the filling.

The bread crumbs absorb the humidity from the cherries.

FLANK WITH FRUITS

French dough (raw)..5.3 kg
Vanilla cream...5kg
Raspberries, blueberries, Strawberries.......6kg
grapes, peaches, apricots...........................8kg
fruits jam...3.2kg

Preparation: spread the French dough in a sheet of 1cm thickness. With a warm knife cut rectangular pieces of 10x6cm. Set them on a tray that was sprinkled with water. Wash them with egg wash. Add a strip of 1cm width to all sides of the rectangle pieces. Pierce each piece in the middle before putting them in the oven. After baking, pour the vanilla cream in the hole and add fruits in top of it. Top them with fruits jam.

PIE WITH VANILLA CREAM

Result 100 pieces of 125g

French dough (raw).....................................4.2kg
Vanilla cream...11kg
powder sugar 400g

Preparation: *Spread the French dough in a sheet of 1/2cm thickness, and set in a tray that was sprinkled with water. Pock it with a fork the entire surface. Bake it at a good heat.*

Set the sheet on a special frame. Cut it in square and pour the vanilla cream hot (see the semi- fabricate chapter). Set the second sheet in top of it and let it cool. Cut it with a wet knife and serve it with powder sugar.

CRÈME SNIT WITH WIPED CREAM AND CACAO

Result 100 pieces of 100g each

For the French dough

Butter	1.250kg
Flour	1.9kg
Salt	50g

For décor

Wiped cream	2.5kg
Sugar	250g
Vanillin	1/4g
Cacao	100g

for cream

sugar	1.4kg
eggs	28 each
flour	800g
milk	4l
vanilla baton	1 each
candied oranges	800g

Preparation: *prepare the French dough and spread it in sheets. After they are baked, set one sheet in a tray and cut it in squares. Set the frame in top and pour the hot vanilla cream (mix the cubed candied fruits to the vanilla cream). Level it and let it cool off.*

Whipped up the cream and add ¾ of the cacao quantity. Spread it evenly over the vanilla cream. Add the second French dough sheet and cut it in squares. Ornate each square with a dollop of whipped cream and powder it with cacao.

MILLES FEUILLES

Butter	*1.6kg*
Flour	*1.9kg*
Salt	*50g*
vinegar	*15ml*
jam	*4.8kg*
sugar	*200g*

Preparation: *prepare the French dough; spread it in sheets of 2-3mm thickness. Set it in trays, pock them and bake them. Cut the sheets in strips of 8-10cm and take 3-4 strips and fill it with jam (smear jam of the surface and the edges of each strip). Warm the fondant and draw strips on top. Let it cool off and cut it in portions.*

MERENGUE WITH JAM

Result 100 pieces of 120g each

French dough baked...................................... 2.3kg
Eggs (34 eggs whites)................................... 17 each
Sugar... 2kg
Prune jam... 4.3kg
strawberry jam 1.450kg
lemon salt... 20g
red color 2g
powder sugar 150g
Strawberry essence....................................... 150g

Preparation: Mix the eggs whites with the sugar, the gem, the strawberry essence, the color, and the lemon salt until the sugar is dissolved. Beat it up with the mixer until it forms hard picks and form the merengue.

Set the baked dough on a wooden plateau and cut it in square pieces. Pour on top of each square the merengue with the posh and dui and level it. Add a curl of merengue in top and serve it with powder sugar.

FRENCH DOUGH POCKETS

Butter...1.9kg
Flour 3.11kg
Pecans..400g
Sugar..1.6kg
Salt..20g
Vinegar 10g
condensed milk..480g
vanillin 5g
eggs..24 each
raisins 200g
rom...100ml
wiped cream...2.5kg

Preparation: prepare the French dough, spread it in a sheet of 1/2cm thickness, wash it with egg wash and cut it with a warm knife in squares.

Fold the square in two, without pressing and set them in a tray that was sprinkled with water. Wash the surface with egg wash and sprinkle chopped pecans on top of them. Bake them first at a good fire then at medium heat. Let them cool off and fill them with vanilla cream mixed with raisins, then wiped cream. Serve them with powder sugar.

ROLLS WITH WIPED CREAM

Result 100 pieces of 60g each.

Butter.. 1.4kg
Flour 1.8kg
Wiped cream.. 2kg
Vinegar.. 20ml
sugar 800g
eggs... 2 each
vanillin.. 1/2g
salt... 50g

Preparation: *prepare the French dough and spread it in a sheet of 1cm thickness. Cut it in strips of 30cm length and 2cm width. Roll them in spiral on special metallic cylindrical forms of 15cm length.*

Wash them with egg wash and sprinkle with sugar. Set them on a try (with the metallic forms inside) and bake them at a good fire. Take them out of the cylinder forms and let them cool off. Fill them with wiped cream that was mixed with sugar and vanilla aroma.